Lady Liberty
and the
Mysterious
Letter

Written by Deborah Dumas

Illustrated by Geoff Schumpert

To Joseph C. Godfrey, Jr.,
thank you for the inspiration.

Daddy got a letter today?
What does it say?
And why is it causing
him to act this way?

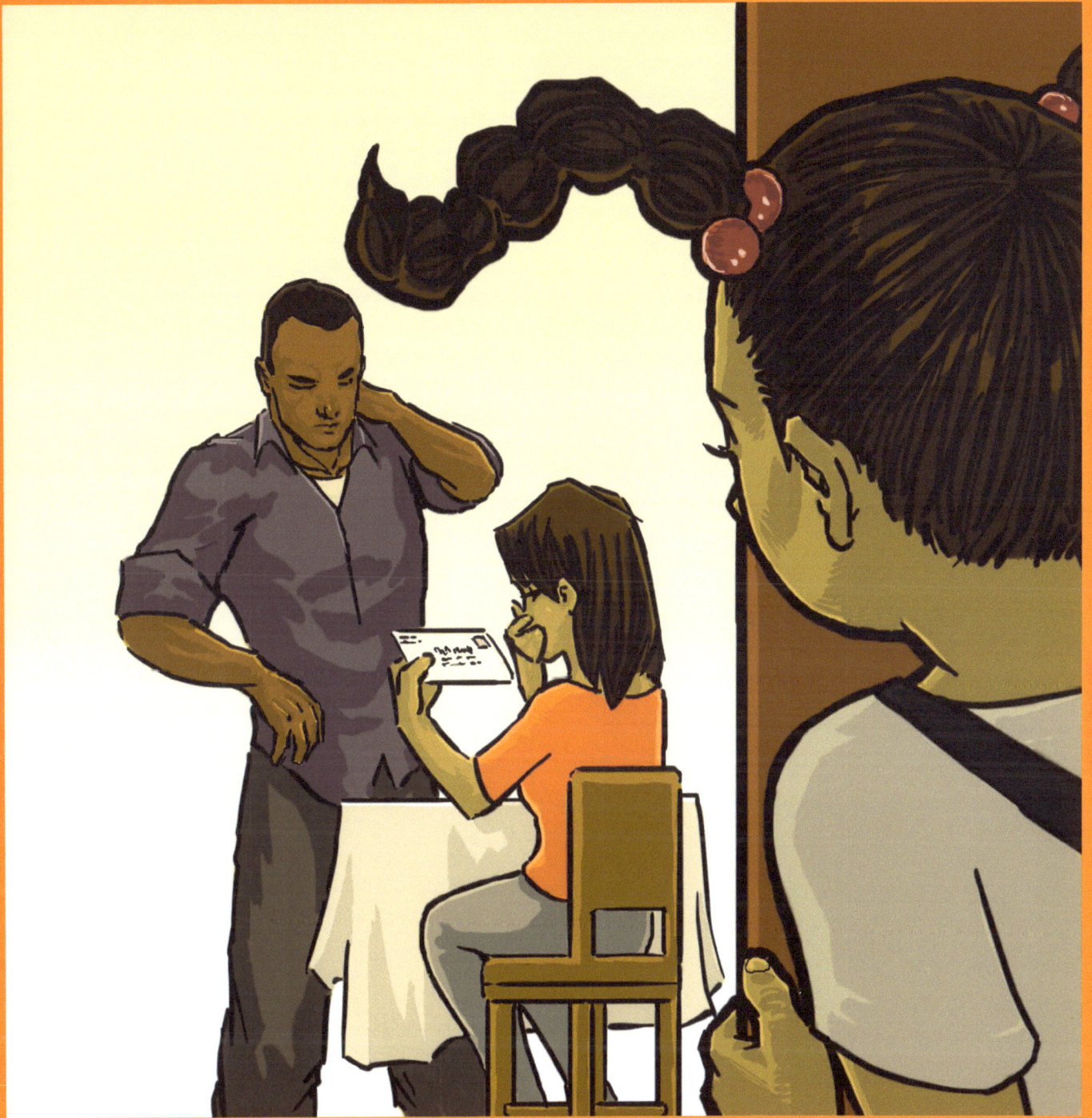

What is happening?
What is going on?
I'm trying to figure out,
why mommy's face is so long?

Is it good news or bad news?
I really don't know.
I guess it's for them to decide,
and them alone.

Uh Oh! Is it about me?

I heard them say my name...

and my name is Lady Liberty.

Am I the one to blame?

"Should we tell her?" Mommy told Daddy.

"We have to!" Daddy replied.

"But we mustn't say it sadly,

or else she might cry."

"It's the right thing to do..." He said,

"don't you understand?

If I tell her to her face,

I will be a better man."

"It's funny," I thought.

What one letter can do.

Is it good news or bad news?

How can I choose?

Overseas?!

What does that mean?

Can somebody tell me

pretty, pretty, please?

Flying planes and helping the country,

That sounds very cool.

I'm thinking too much again,

I just want to throw all of

my thoughts into the pool.

I heard them say a week.

A week is all we got.

Then daddy will have to leave,

whether we like it or not.

"How long have you been
standing there, Liberty?
I think you heard it all.
Well, it doesn't matter anyway.
For our time is very small."

He said:

GRAB YOUR SKATES

WE'LL HAVE A RACE!

GRAB THAT BAT

27

AND MOVE THAT CAT!

LET'S GO DANCE!

31

WE'LL PRANCE, PRANCE, PRANCE!

WE'LL GO TO THE BEACH

ON THE WAY WE'LL
HAVE A TREAT.

OR DO YOU WANT TO
GO TO THE PARK?

OR GO SEE WORKS OF ART?

"Sure!" I said.

And let's take pictures!

Pictures by the fixtures
And pictures by the sled.

But then the day was over
So he put me to bed.

Morning came and
Daddy's bags were packed.
He said, "I love you,
Lady Liberty and that's a fact!"

Is it good news or bad news?

How can I choose?

But the memories I have of Daddy,

I'll never lose.

www.ingramcontent.com/pod-product-compliance
Lightning Source LLC
LaVergne TN
LVHW072129070426

835513LV00002B/42